Student Guidebook to Proper Citation in APA Style

Taken from:

Prentice Hall Reference Guide, Sixth Edition
by Muriel Harris

PEARSON
Custom
Publishing

PEARSON
Prentice
Hall

Cover Art: *Untitled #50*, by Glenn Kremer

Taken from:

Prentice Hall Reference Guide, Sixth Edition
by Muriel Harris
Copyright © 2006, 2003, 2000, 1997, 1994, 1991
by Pearson Education, Inc.
Published by Prentice Hall
Upper Saddle River, New Jersey, 07458

Printed in the United States of America

10 9 8 7 6 5 4 3 2

ISBN 0-536-31641-4

2006240474

EM

Please visit our web site at *www.pearsoncustom.com*

PEARSON CUSTOM PUBLISHING
75 Arlington Street, Suite 300, Boston, MA 02116
A Pearson Education Company

APA DOCUMENTATION

CONTENTS

APA DOCUMENTATION

Other Sources 13

1
DOCUMENTING IN APA STYLE

The format prescribed by the **American Psychological Association (APA)** is used to document papers in the fields of psychology, sociology, business, economics, nursing, social work, and criminology. Ask for your instructor's preference. If you are asked to use APA format, follow the guidelines offered here and consult the *Publication Manual of the American Psychological Association* (5th ed., Washington, D.C.: American Psychological Association, 2001). Check for updates on the APA Web site, **www.apastyle.org**.

APA style is like MLA style in that it uses parenthetical citations to refer readers to a list of sources at the end of the paper and that numbered notes may be used to give information that would disrupt the flow of the writing. The list of works cited, headed "References," includes all the sources mentioned in the body of the paper. APA style differs from MLA style in other respects, however. For example, APA style includes the date of publication in parenthetical citations, and the date appears after the author's name in the References. In addition, authors' first and middle names are indicated by initials only. Capitalization and use of quotation marks and italics also differ in APA style.

The following are some features of APA style:

♦ The paper begins with a brief abstract or summary.

♦ For in-text citations, give the author's last name and the publication year of the source.

♦ In quotations, put signal words in past tense ("Smith reported") or present perfect tense ("as Smith has reported").

♦ In the References list at the end of the paper, give full publication information, alphabetized by author.

♦ Use full last names but only initials of first and middle names of authors.

♦ Capitalize only the first word and proper names in book and article titles, but capitalize all major words in journal titles. Use italics for book and journal titles; do not put article titles in quotation marks.

♦ Use the ampersand (&) instead of the word *and* with authors' names in parenthetical citations, tables, captions, and the References.

1a   In-Text Citations

When you use APA format and refer to sources in your text, include the author's name and date of publication. For direct quotations, include the page number also.

EXAMPLES OF APA IN-TEXT CITATIONS

1. Direct quotations
2. Author's name given in the text
3. Author's name not given in the text
4. Work by multiple authors
5. Group as author
6. Unknown author
7. Authors with the same last name
8. Two or more works in the same citation
9. Biblical and classical works
10. Specific parts of a source
11. Personal communications
12. World Wide Web

---

1. Direct Quotations When you quote a source, end with quotation marks and give the author, year, and page number in parentheses.

> Many others agree with the assessment that "this is a seriously flawed study" (Methasa, 1994, p. 22) and do not include its data in their own work.

2. Author's Name Given in the Text Cite only the year of publication in parentheses.

> When Millard (1970) compared reaction times among the participants, he noticed an increase in errors.

If the year appears in the sentence, do not add parenthetical information. If you refer to the same study again in the paragraph, with the source's name, you do not have to cite the year again if it is clear that the same study is being referred to.

> In 1994, Pradha found improvement in short-term memory with accompanying practice.

3. Author's Name Not Given in the Text Cite the name and year, separated by a comma.

> In a recent study of reaction times (Millard, 1970), no change was noticed.

4. Work by Multiple Authors For two authors, cite both names every time you refer to the source. Use *and* in the text, but use an ampersand (&) in parenthetical material, tables, captions, and the References list.

When Glick and Metah (1991) reported on their findings, they were unaware of a similar study (Grimm & Tolman, 1991) with contradictory data.

For three, four, or five authors, include all authors (and date) the first time you cite the source. For additional references to the same work, use only the first author's name and *et al.* (for "and others"), with no underlining or italics.

Ellison, Mayer, Brunerd, and Keif (1987) studied supervisors who were given no training.

Later, when Ellison et al. (1987) continued their study of these same supervisors, they added a one-week training program.

For six or more authors, cite only the first author and *et al.* and the year for all references.

Mokach et al. (1989) noted no improvement in norms for participant scores.

5. Group as Author The name of the group that serves as the author (for example, a government agency or a corporation) is usually spelled out every time it appears in a citation. If the name is long but easily identified by its abbreviation and you want to switch to the abbreviation, give the abbreviation in parentheses when the entire name first appears.

In 1992, when the National Institutes of Mental Health (NIMH) prepared its report, no field data on this epidemic were available. However, NIMH agreed that future reports would correct this deficiency.

6. Unknown Author When a work has no author indicated, cite the first few words of the title and the year.

One newspaper article ("When South Americans," 1987) indicated the rapid growth of this phenomenon.

7. Authors with the Same Last Name If two or more authors listed in the References have the same last name, include their initials in all text citations.

Until T. A. Wilman (1994) studied the initial survey (M. R. Wilman, 1993), no reports were issued.

8. Two or More Works in the Same Citation When two or more works are cited within the same parentheses, arrange them in the order in which they appear in the References list, and separate them with semicolons.

Several studies (Canin, 1989; Duniere, 1987; Pferman & Chu, 1991) reported similar behavior patterns in such cases.

9. Biblical and Classical Works Reference entries are not necessary for major classical works such as the Bible and ancient Greek and Roman works, but identify the version you used in the first citation in your text. If appropriate, in each citation, include the part (book, chapter, lines).

When Abraham saw three men passing his tent, he asked them to stop and not

pass by him (Gen. 18:3, Revised Standard Version).

This was known (Aristotle, trans. 1931) to be prevalent among young men with

these symptoms.

10. Specific Parts of a Source To cite a specific part of a source, include the page, chapter, figure, or table, and use the abbreviations *p.* (for "page") and *chap.* (for "chapter").

No work was done on interaction of long-term memory and computer

programming (Sitwa & Shiu, 1993, p. 224), but recently Takamuru (1996,

chap. 6) reported studies that have considered this interaction.

For an electronic source that contains no page number, cite the paragraph number with the paragraph symbol (¶) or abbreviation for paragraph (*para.*). When no paragraph number is given, cite the heading and the number of the paragraph following it.

The two methods showed a significant difference (Smith, 2000, ¶ 2) when

repeated with a different age group.

No further study indicated any change in the results (Thomasus, 2001,

Conclusion, para. 3).

11. Personal Communications Personal communications include letters, memos, telephone conversations, and electronic communications such as e-mail, discussion groups, and messages on electronic bulletin boards that are not archived. Because the data cannot be recovered, these are included only in the text and not in the References list. Include the initials and last name of the communicator and as exact a date as possible. (For electronic sources that can be documented, see 1c.)

According to I. M. Boza (personal communication, June 18, 1995), no population

studies of the problem were done before 1993.

12. World Wide Web To cite a Web site in the text (but not a specific document), include the Web address. See 1c for more information.

Consult the Web site for the American Psychological Association (http://www.apastyle.org) for updates on how to cite Internet sources.

1b   Footnotes

In your paper, you may need footnotes to expand on content and to acknowledge copyrighted material. Content footnotes add important information that cannot be integrated into the text, but they are distracting and should be used only if they strengthen the discussion. Copyright permission footnotes acknowledge the source of quotations and other materials that are copyrighted. Number the footnotes consecutively with superscript arabic numerals, and include the footnotes on a separate page after the References list.

1c   References List

Arrange all entries in alphabetical order by the author's last name; for several works by one author, arrange by year of publication with the earliest one first. For authors' names, give all surnames first and then the initials. Use commas to separate a list of two or more names, and use an ampersand (&) before the last name in the list. Capitalize only the first word of the title and the subtitle (and any proper names) of a book or article, but capitalize all main words in the name of the journal. Italicize book titles, names of journals, and the volume number of the journal. For each entry in the list, the first line begins at the left margin and all following lines are indented five spaces.

EXAMPLES OF APA REFERENCES
Books

1. One author
2. Two or more works by the same author
3. Two or more authors
4. Group or corporate author
5. Unknown author
6. Edited volume
7. Translation
8. Article or chapter in an edited book
9. Article in a reference book
10. Revised edition
11. Book, later edition
12. Multivolume work
13. Technical or research report
14. Report from a university
15. Biblical and classical works

EXAMPLES OF APA REFERENCES

Articles in Periodicals

16. Article in a journal paginated continuously
17. Article in a journal paginated separately by issue
18. Article in a magazine
19. Article in a newspaper
20. Unsigned article
21. Monograph
22. Review of a book
23. Review of a motion picture
24. Letter to the editor

Electronic Sources

25. Journal article
26. Article in an Internet-only journal
27. Newspaper article
28. Online article from a database
29. Chapter or section in an Internet document
30. Stand-alone document, no author identified, no date
31. Abstract
32. U.S. government report available on the Web
33. Web page, untitled
34. Web page, review of a motion picture
35. Message posted to a newsgroup
36. Message posted to an electronic mailing list
37. E-mail
38. Electronic database
39. CD-ROM
40. DVD
41. Computer program or software

Other Sources

42. Information service
43. Dissertation abstract
44. Government document
45. Conference proceedings
46. Interview
47. Motion picture released theatrically
48. Videotape, performance, or artwork
49. Audio recording
50. Television series
51. Episode from a television series
52. Radio broadcast
53. Unpublished paper presented at a meeting

Start the References list on a new page, with the word *References* centered at the top of the page, and double-space all entries.

Books

1. One Author

Cleary, B. L. (2004). *Conducting research in long-term care settings.*

New York: Springer.

2. Two or More Works by the Same Author
Include the author's name in all references and arrange by year of publication, the earliest first.

Kilmonto, R. J. (1983). *Culture and ethnicity.* Washington, DC:

American Psychiatric Press.

Kilmonto, R. J. (1989). *Cultural adaptations.* New York:

HarperCollins.

3. Two or More Authors

Aronson, E., Wilson, T. D., & Akers, R. M. (2004). *Social Psychology*

(4th ed.). Upper Saddle River, NJ: Prentice Hall.

4. Group or Corporate Author
If the publication is a brochure, indicate that in brackets.

Mental Health Technical Training Support Center. (1994).

Guidelines for mental health nonprofit agency staffs (2nd ed.)

[Brochure]. Manhattan, KS: Author.

5. Unknown Author

Americana collegiate dictionary (4th ed.). (1995). Indianapolis, IN:

Huntsfield.

6. Edited Volume

D'Agata, J. (Ed.). (2003). *The next American essay.* Saint Paul, MN:

Graywolf Press.

7. Translation

Lefranc, J. R. (1976). *A treatise on probability* (R. W. Mateau &

D. Trilling, Trans.). New York: Macmillan. (Original work

published 1952)

8. Article or Chapter in an Edited Book

Riesen, A. H. (1991). Sensory deprivation. In E. Stellar & J. M.

Sprague (Eds.), *Progress in physiological psychology*

(pp. 24–54). New York: Academic Press.

9. Article in a Reference Book

Terusami, H. T. (1993). Relativity. In *The new handbook of science* (Vol. 12, pp. 247–249). Chicago: Modern Science.

10. Revised Edition

Telphafi, J. (1989). *Diagnostic techniques* (Rev. ed.). Newbury Park, CA: Pine Forge Press.

11. Book, Later Edition

Hauser, G. A. (2003). *Introduction to rhetorical theory* (2nd ed.). Prospect Heights, IL: Waveland Press.

12. Multivolume Work

Donovan, W. (Ed.). (1979–1986). *Social sciences: A history* (Vols. 1–5). New York: Hollins.

13. Technical or Research Report

Birney, A. F., & Hall, M. M. (1981). *Early identification of children with written language disabilities* (Rep. No. 81-502). Washington, DC: National Education Association.

14. Report from a University

Lundersen, P. S., McIver, R. L., & Yepperman, B. B. (1990). *Sexual harassment policies and the law* (Tech. Rep. No. 9). Springfield: University of Central Indiana, Faculty Affairs Research Center.

15. Biblical and Classical Works Major classical works, such as the Bible and ancient Greek and Roman works, are not listed in the References. Instead, they are cited in the paper when referred to. See 1a for in-text citation format and examples.

Articles in Periodicals

16. Article in a Journal Paginated Continuously

Schaubroeck, J., Sime, W. E., & Mayes, B. T. (1991). The nomological validity of the Type A personality. *Journal of Applied Psychology, 76,* 143–168.

17. Article in a Journal Paginated Separately by Issue

Timmo, L. A., & Kikovio, R. (1994). Young children's attempts at deception. *Research in Early Childhood Learning, 53*(2), 49–67.

18. Article in a Magazine

Vidal, G. (2003, June 2). We are all patriots. *Nation, 276,* 11–15.

19. Article in a Newspaper For newspaper articles, use *p.* or *pp.* before the page numbers.

> Banerjee, N. (2004, September 1). Many feeling pinch after newest
>
> surge in U.S. fuel prices. *The New York Times,* p. A1.

20. Unsigned Article

> New study promises age-defying pills. (1995, July 27). *The*
>
> *Washington Post,* p. B21.

21. Monograph

> Rotter, P. B., & Stolz, G. (1966). Generalized expectancies of early
>
> childhood speech patterns. *Monographs of the Childhood*
>
> *Education Society, 36*(2, Serial No. 181).

22. Review of a Book

> Hahn, U., & Zorzi, M. (2004). Charting human perceptual changes
>
> [Review of the book *Cognitive dynamics: Conceptual and*
>
> *representational change in humans and machines*]. *European*
>
> *Journal of Cognitive Psychology, 16,* 473–478.

If the review is untitled, use the material in brackets as the title and indicate whether the review is of a book, film, or video; the brackets indicate the material is a description of form and content, not a title.

23. Review of a Motion Picture

> Veltman, C. (2004). [Review of the motion picture *Super Size Me*].
>
> *British Medical Journal, 328,* 1266.

24. Letter to the Editor

> Strader, L. (2004, June 7). What hypocrisy! [Letter to the editor].
>
> *Forbes, 173*(12), 30.

Electronic Sources

The APA has posted guidelines on its Web site (www.apastyle.org) for citing information from the Internet. The goal of each reference is to credit the author and to help your reader find the material. However, sources may lack some of the information needed. But at a minimum, include document title or description, a date (date of publication, update, or retrieval), and the address (the uniform resource locator, or URL). If possible, include the author of the document. It is always important to note the date you retrieved the document from the Internet because the content may change, be revised, or be removed.

If you have to divide the address so that it starts on one line and continues on the next, break the address before a period or after a slash, and never add a hyphen. Write the URL like the rest of your text; do not use underlining, italics, angle brackets, or an end period.

25. Journal Article If the article appears online exactly as it appears in the print source, use the following format:

> Majitsu, J. (2001). Necessary intervention in teenage depression
>
> [Electronic version]. *Behavior Intervention, 6,* 36–54.

If you read an article online from a print source but you think the online version may have been revised, or if you notice that the format differs from the print source or page numbers are not indicated, use the following format:

> Klein, D. F. (1997). Control groups in pharmacotherapy and
>
> psychotherapy evaluations. *Treatment, 1,* Article 1. Retrieved
>
> February 9, 2002, from http://journals.apa.org/treatment/vol1/
>
> 97_a1.html

26. Article in an Internet-Only Journal (For articles retrieved via file transfer protocol [FTP], use that URL.)

> Greenberg, M. T., Domitrovich C., & Bumbarger, B. (2001, March 30).
>
> The prevention of mental disorders in school-aged children:
>
> Current state of the field. *Prevention and Treatment, 4.*
>
> Retrieved July 18, 2001, from http://journals.apa.org/prevention/
>
> volume4/pre0040001a.html

27. Newspaper Article

> Kass, J. (2004, June 3). Fugitive's arrest in Mexico hits close to City
>
> Hall. *Chicago Tribune.* Retrieved June 3, 2004, from http://www
>
> .chicagotribune.com/news/columnists/

28. Online Article from a Database

> Beinart, P. (2004, May 31). Outsourcing. *New Republic, 230*(20), 6.
>
> Retrieved June 3, 2004, from Academic Search Elite database.

29. Chapter or Section in an Internet Document

> Berwick, D. M. (1999). As good as it should get: Making health care
>
> better in the new millennium. In *Policy studies, national*
>
> *coalition on health care* (sec. Adding it up). Retrieved August
>
> 1, 2001, from http://www.nchc.org/berwick.html#ADDING

30. Stand-Alone Document, No Author Identified, No Date

Associative learning. (n.d.). Retrieved July 18, 2001, from http://
psy.soton.ac.uk/RGdata/lbarg/Associative%20Learning.htm

31. Abstract

Dukas, R. (2001). *Effects of perceived danger on flower choice by
bees.* Abstract retrieved July 18, 2001, from http://
www.sfu.ca/biology/faculty/dukas/abstracts.htm#hbpred

32. U.S. Government Report Available on the Web

National Institutes of Health. (2001). *Stem cells: Scientific progress
and future research.* Retrieved July 19, 2001, from http://
www.nih.gov/news/stemcell/scireport.htm

33. Web Page, Untitled

Carver College of Medicine. (2004). Home page. Retrieved June 3,
2004, from University of Iowa Web site: http://
www.medicine.uiowa.edu/

34. Web Page, Review of a Motion Picture

Lehmann, M. (2004, May 28). Brain-freezing fun [Review of the motion
picture *The day after tomorrow*]. Retrieved May 31, 2004, from
http://www.nypost.com/movies/21783.htm

35. Message Posted to a Newsgroup

Woodgate, J. (2001, July 16). Calif. to change their voltage? [Msg. 1].
Message posted to news://sci.electronics.design

36. Message Posted to an Electronic Mailing List

Wood, E. (2000, October 5). Re: Basic Citation Tags. Message posted
to LegalXML Citations Workgroup Listserv mailing list,
archived at http://camlaw.rutgers.edu/~jjoerg/citations/1.id

37. E-Mail Personal e-mail and other electronic communications that
are not archived are identified as personal communications in the paper
and are not listed in the References list.

38. Electronic Database

Center for Public Policy Study. (1994). *Survey of public response to terrorism abroad, 1992–93.* Retrieved October 20, 1994, from USGOV database.

39. CD-ROM

Culrose, P., Trimmer, N., & Debruikker, K. (1996). Gender differentiation in fear responses [CD-ROM]. *Emotion and Behavior, 27,* 914–937. Abstract retrieved July 7, 1997, from FirstSearch (PsycLIT Item: 900312) database.

40. DVD

Daldry, S. (Director), Rudin, S., Fox, R. (Producers), & Hare, D. (Writer). (2003). *The hours* [DVD]. United States: Paramount Home Entertainment. (Original release date 2002)

See entry 46 for motion pictures viewed in a theater.

41. Computer Program or Software

Gangnopahdhav, A. (1994). *Data analyzer for e-mail usage* [Computer software]. Princeton, NJ: MasterMinders.

Other Sources

42. Information Service

Mead, J. V. (1992). *Looking at old photographs: Investigating the teacher tales that novice teachers bring with them* (Report No. NCRTL-RR-92-4). East Lansing, MI: National Center for Research on Teacher Learning. (ERIC Document Reproduction Service No. ED346082)

43. Dissertation Abstract

Rosen, P. R. (1994). Learning to cope with family crises through counselor mediation (Doctoral dissertation, Claremont University, 1994). *Dissertation Abstracts International, 53,* Z6812.

44. Government Document

Environmental Protection Agency. (2003). *Protect your family from lead in your home* (Publication No. EPA 747-K-99-001). Washington, DC: U.S. Government Printing Office.

45. Conference Proceedings

> Cordulla, F. M., Teitelman, P. J., & Preba, E. E. (1995). Biofeedback in
> muscle relaxation. *Proceedings of the National Academy of*
> *Biological Sciences, USA, 96,* 1271–1342.

46. Interview Personal interviews are not included in the References list. Instead, use a parenthetical citation in the text. List published interviews under the interviewer's name.

> Daly, C. C. (1995, July 14). [Interview with Malcolm Forbes].
> *International Business Weekly, 37,* 34–35.

47. Motion Picture Released Theatrically

> Dannelly, B. (Writer/Director), Urban, M. (Writer). Stipe, M., Stern S.,
> Vince, W., & Ohoven, M. (Producers). (2004). *Saved!* [Motion
> picture]. United States: United Artists.

See entry 39 for motion pictures viewed on DVD.

48. Videotape, Performance, or Artwork Start with the name and, in parentheses, functions of the originators or primary contributors. Put the medium in brackets after the title. Give the name and location of the distributor, and if the company is not well known, include the address.

> Weiss, I. (Producer), & Terris, A. (Director). (1992). *Infant babbling*
> *and speech production* [Videotape]. (Available from Childhood
> Research Foundation, 125 Marchmont Avenue, Suite 224, New
> York, NY 10022)

49. Audio Recording

> Sedaris, D. (Speaker). (2003, October 9). *David Sedaris live at*
> *Carnegie Hall* [CD]. New York: Little, Brown.

50. Television Series Start with the name, and then in parentheses the person's function (for example, *Producer*), and insert a period. Then include the date in parentheses, a period, and the title, followed by *Television broadcast* enclosed in brackets, a period, the place the broadcast originated from, a colon, and the broadcasting network.

> Wells, J., Crichton, M., Baer, N., & Orman, J. (Producers). (2004). *ER*
> [Television broadcast]. New York: NBC.

51. Episode from a Television Series

> Shankar, N. (Writer), & Fink, K. (Director). (2004, June 3). Paper or
> plastic? [Television series episode]. In Bruckheimer, J.,

Mendelsohn, C., Donahue, A., Zuiker, A., Petersen, W. (Producers), *CSI: Crime scene investigation.* New York: CBS.

52. Radio Broadcast

Amari, C., & Wolski, R. (Producers). (2004, May 29). *Twilight time* [Radio program]. Chicago: WGN Radio.

53. Unpublished Paper Presented at a Meeting

Lillestein, M. A. (1994, January 20). *Notes on interracial conflict in college settings.* Paper presented at the meeting of the American Cultural Studies Society, San Antonio, TX.

1d   Sample APA-Style Research Paper

A sample student research paper using APA format and documentation begins on the next page. For all pages, leave a margin of at least one inch on all sides.

Intercountry Adoption   1

Running head: INTERCOUNTRY ADOPTION FROM CHINA   **1**

Intercountry Adoption from China

Jamie Anderson

University of Delaware   **2**

(Proportions shown in the margins of the APA paper are not actual but have been adjusted to fit space limitations of this book. Follow actual dimensions indicated and your instructor's directions.)

Comments

1 The title page has a running head typed in capital letters at top left (specifically to be used for publication purposes). Note that for all research papers, the entire essay has an abbreviated running head (in this case "Intercountry Adoption") in a header with the page number, justified to the right margin.

2 The title, byline (writer's name), and affiliation (writer's college) are double-spaced and centered on the page. According to the APA manual, this information is all that is required for a professional publication. Many instructors prefer that you include the title, your name, instructor's name, course, and date instead so check with your instructor.

Abstract

3

Adoption of children from other countries by American families has grown dramatically since World War II, and in the past decade, adoptions of Chinese children have risen from a few hundred to over 5,000. Studies on the effects of intercountry adoption from China reveal both positive and negative results. Negatives include identity confusion, racism, and developmental delays. With understanding and support, however, adoptive parents can overcome these obstacles. In addition to published research, personal experiences of real adoptive families are cited. Intercountry adoption is found to be a generally positive experience for both parents and children.

4

Comments

> **3** The second page of the essay begins with an abstract. Note the title (Abstract), centered at the top of the page.

> **4** The abstract should summarize an essay briefly (in about one hundred words) and accurately. Major assertions and research findings should be stated.

Intercountry Adoption   3

Intercountry Adoption from China   **5**

Intercountry adoption, the process of adopting children from across international borders, has been taking place since the years immediately following World War II. From that point forward, intercountry adoption became a well-known practice, occurring in many countries for various reasons. It has been continuing to grow in popularity in the United States for years now. According to Rojewski and Rojewski (2001), there were 7,948 intercountry   **6**
adoptions in the United States in 1989; in 1998, that number rose to 15,774, accounting for 12% to 13% of all adoptions (p. 3). Even more   **7**
impressive has been the extreme growth in number of adoptions from China. In 1992, only 201 children were brought into the United States from China. By 2000, that number had grown to 5,053 children (p. 3). Although extensive research is still being conducted   **8**
regarding the process and effects of intercountry adoption from China, many studies have already been completed. These studies have revealed a variety of results, both positive and negative. It has become apparent that while the effects of intercountry adoption from China are far-reaching for both the adoptee and the adoptive parents, there is no reason why intercountry adoption from China should be opposed.   **9**

When intercountry adoption first began to occur after World War II, it was generally done for humanitarian reasons. The first   **10**
children to be adopted internationally were European orphans. This also occurred after both the Korean War in the 1950s and the Vietnam War in the 1970s (Rojewski & Rojewski, 2001, p. 2).   **11**
Triseliotis (1993) suggests that the motive for intercountry adoption at these times was mostly to rescue the children who were negatively affected by the wars going on in their native countries.

Comments

5 The title of the essay is repeated on the third page, centered.

6 APA style favors signal phrases using authors' names, always followed by the date of publication of the source being cited.

7 Parenthetical page references in APA style require the abbreviation *p.* before the page number. Note also that if a signal phrase is used, the name may be omitted from the page reference.

8 Within the same paragraph, if the source being cited is the same as the previous source, only the page number need be given.

9 It is clear from this thesis that while the essay will address both positives and negatives of adoption of Chinese children into the United States, it will conclude that the practice should continue.

10 Here begins a section that sketches the history of intercountry adoption and accounts for its growing popularity.

11 If no signal phrase is used, authors' names, publication dates, and page numbers go in parentheses, separated by commas. Note that an ampersand (&) replaces the word *and* in a parenthetical citation.

Today, however, the most common reason for intercountry adoption is for childless couples to become parents. There is a general lack of availability of white American children up for adoption, so couples turn to international adoption to fill the void.

There are even more specific reasons as to why China has become such a popular place from which to adopt. Even in the early 1990s, adoption from China was extremely rare. Tessler, Gamache, and Liu (1999) note that in 1992, the People's Republic of China passed an adoption law, formalizing the process of intercountry adoption from China. The biggest reason for this growth in popularity is the abundance of children, mostly girls, available to adopt from China. In 1979, a one-child-per-couple policy was implemented by the Chinese government. The law, intended to help control the ever-growing Chinese population, stated that there was a strict one-child policy in urban areas and a "one-son/two-child" rule in rural parts of the country (Rojewski & Rojewski, 2001, p. 5). Since the implementation of this law, hundreds of thousands of baby girls have been abandoned each year, for the most part because of the long-standing social preference for sons. Sons are able to carry on the family name, can perform heavier workloads, and are responsible for caring for their parents when they reach old age. For these reasons, among others, as Bazzoli (2002) notes, 92 percent of the children abandoned in China are girls, making the vast majority of babies adopted from China female (p. 3).

12

Although child abandonment, and therefore availability, is most responsible for the growth in popularity of Chinese adoptions, other reasons contribute to the practice. Tessler et al. (1999) note that "eligibility, health status of prospective children,

13

Comments

12 Note in this paragraph the skillful use of three different sources to offer a coherent reason for the growth in adoption of Chinese children.

13 If a work has three or more authors, all authors (up to five) are named in the first citation of the work, but only the first author's name, followed by *et al.,* is used thereafter. (If a work has six or more authors, the form using *et al.* is used for all citations, including the first.)

Intercountry Adoption   5

and cultural and personal interests may all be involved . . .
in leading one to adopt from China" (pp. 79–80). Adoption
requirements are also less strict than those regarding adoptions
in the United States. Prospective adoptive parents of Chinese
children can be married or single, but they must be at least
35 years of age and childless. The adoption process itself is also
favored because it is fairly short, only around 18 months, and there
is an extremely slim chance that birth parents would ever return
for their child in the future (Bazzoli, 2002, p. 5).

Due to the fact that intercountry adoption from China is a
relatively new practice, many studies are still under way to learn
the effects that this type of adoption has on the adopted children,
as well as the adoptive families. Enough research has been done
already, however, for experts to determine whether to oppose or
support the practice of intercountry adoption from China.   **14**

The majority of those who are opposed cite racial and cultural
differences as their biggest concern. Intercountry adoptees can feel
caught between two identities. Are they American, Chinese, or
both? Integrating the two cultures can be a very difficult process,
one that some fear the adoptive parents do not recognize at the
time of adoption. Tessler et al. (1999) agree that "the most negative
potential outcome of bicultural socialization is that children
develop no strong attachment to either culture, thus feeling
isolated and alone, without a strong reference group" (p. 25).
Another reason cited in opposition to intercountry adoption is
that the adopted child will be more susceptible to racism. This is
another area that many adoptive parents are not well equipped
to deal with. Finally, developmental delays are likely in
internationally adopted children. Whether in speech and mental

Comments

14 This transitional paragraph signals the end of the section on the history of intercountry adoption and the beginning of a new section that addresses more directly the thesis from the end of the first paragraph about the advisability of intercountry adoption.

Intercountry Adoption   6

capabilities or other medical conditions, such as height and
weight, "as many as three-fourths of all Chinese adoptees
experience some type of developmental delay for a period
of time after adoption" (Rojewski & Rojewski, 2001, p. 61).

15

Many of the people who support intercountry adoption from
China have personal experience in the area. Conclusive studies
done back up their beliefs. One study cited by Vonk (2002)
concluded that "in 75%–80% of intercountry adoptions the children
and adolescents function well, with no more behavioral and
educational problems at home and at school than other children,
and . . . they have close and mutually satisfying relationships with
their parents" (p. 4). Researchers have not been able to find
substantial evidence that children adopted internationally are in
any way more likely to encounter educational, social, or emotional
conflicts. Most of the children studied have been able to adjust
quickly to life in their new countries, homes, and families. As for
other reasons to support intercountry adoption, many believe that
by allowing these underprivileged children into the country, more
attention will be given to the fact that there are still thousands of
other children left suffering. Still others believe that it would be
immoral not to allow children to be removed from orphanages and
institutions when there are good homes available for them in other
countries (Triseliotis, 1993). Rojewski and Rojewski (2001) flatly
state, "There is no factual basis for the arguments used to oppose
intercountry adoption. They are without merit" (p. 21).

16

The issue of adjustment is the most discussed variable when
dealing with the support or opposition of intercountry adoption
from China. Intercountry adoption does not only affect the adopted
child but the parents and the rest of the family as well. Before even

17

Comments

15 This paragraph summarizes three strong objections to intercountry adoption. If we remember the general thesis (at the end of paragraph one), we shouldn't be surprised when these objections are addressed later in the essay.

16 This paragraph counters the previous one with reasons in favor of intercountry adoption.

17 The essay returns here to the objections raised in paragraph six. This will occupy the essay for the next eight paragraphs.

considering adopting a child from another country, families need to realize that by adopting a child of a minority ethnicity, the status of the entire family changes to multicultural. According to the National Adoption Information Clearinghouse, "When you adopt a child of another race or culture, it is not only the child who is different. Your family becomes a 'different' family" ("Transracial," 2002, p. 2). Prospective adoptive parents have to think about whether or not extended family members or friends will have any problems accepting their decision to adopt internationally and whether these concerns will affect their opinions. So even though the biggest adjustment awaits the adoptee, the adoptive parents will have many adjustments to deal with as well.

The way parents choose to deal with the integration of the Chinese and American cultures can have a startling influence on the child's overall adjustment process. Some people who oppose intercountry adoption from China believe that for many parents the task is too hard: "Parents must find a difficult balance that neither sets the child apart as being different nor denies the child's origins" (Rojewski & Rojewski, 2001, p. 96). Vonk (2002) concluded that parents need to be educated in the following categories in order to help their internationally adopted child adjust properly: "racial awareness," "survival skills," and "multicultural [family] planning" (p. 8). Racial awareness refers to the degree to which the parents recognize how race affects their own lives and how it will affect the life of their adopted child. Survival skills refer to the skills that parents teach their child about dealing with racism in daily life. It is imperative that adoptees receive the necessary "help to develop strong self-images despite racism" (Vonk, 2002, p. 9). Some techniques include talking openly about racial issues,

Comments

18 An introductory phrase that identifies an expert source in this way can strengthen the effect of the information presented.

practicing answers to potentially harmful comments, and showing no personal tolerance for racist remarks. Multicultural family planning advocates a hands-on approach to helping the child learn more about his or her culture (p. 10).

There are many ways in which parents can help their child achieve the right balance between cultures. Open communication regarding these cultural differences seems to be the most important factor. Children have to be given the liberty to discuss **19** how they feel because they are the ones who actually deal with the effects of bicultural socialization on a daily basis. Another important factor in achieving balance is the incorporation of **20** Chinese culture and heritage in all aspects of the child's life. Suggested ways to do so include acknowledging different facets of Chinese culture, interacting with other Chinese people, and celebrating adoption-related events. According to Dickinson (2002), many families also choose to celebrate native holidays and rituals, such as the Chinese New Year. Parents can help their child interact with other members of their race by joining playgroups that consist of other adoptees, living in culturally diverse neighborhoods, and finding positive role models of Chinese ethnicity. Ways to celebrate adoption-related events consist of including the child's birth name in her newly given American name. Parents can also acknowledge the day that the parents first met the child. This practice, "referred to by many as 'Gotcha Day,' was the most frequently celebrated of all adoption-related events" (Rojewski & Rojewski, 2001, p. 97). By acknowledging the cultural differences in these ways and others, adoptees are likely to develop a deep sense of trust for their parents, positive attitudes toward family members, positive self-esteem, and better reactions toward racism.

Comments

19 Note how the abstract generalization about the need for open communication is followed by a concrete example.

20 Here the author uses the transitional device of repetition in the sentence to repeat the phrase "important factor" introduced earlier in the paragraph.

With the ever-increasing numbers of Chinese children being adopted by U.S. families, the number of support groups for adoptive families is also growing. The largest of these groups is Families with Children from China (FCC). All chapters of this organization have three shared goals: "to support families who've adopted in China," "to encourage adoption from China," and "to advocate for and support children remaining in orphanages in China" (cited in Tessler et al., 1999, p. 61). The FCC holds family **21** picnics, Chinese festivals, and playgroups, among other events, all to help with the adjustment process of the adoptees and their new families.

Even with all of the help from the adoptive parents, adoptees still "must struggle to integrate an identity that includes acceptance of their own physical appearances, their birth heritage, and the heritage of their upbringing" (Vonk, 2002, p. 5). Although intercountry adoptees are forced to make adjustments to deal with these struggles throughout their lives, there are some important steps that normally occur during specific life stages. During infancy, the biggest adjustments for the adoptee are learning to trust and making the transition to a new home and family. Parents are faced with certain adjustment issues at this time as well. They are responsible for building parent-child relationships at this point, along with the job of deciding how cultural heritage will be acknowledged when the time comes. During the toddler and preschool years, the child cannot fully understand what adoption means, but parents need to begin preparing them for this knowledge and how to handle it. The middle years of childhood, between the ages of 6 and 12, are when most adjustment issues surface. Abandonment issues are

Comments

21 Though Anderson is quoting the goals of Families with Children from China, she found the quotations in another source: Tessler, Gamache, and Liu (1999). Note her way of letting the reader know this.

generally discovered for the first time, and "the loss of one's roots and identity may cause the child difficulty in establishing a sense of self and birth heritage" (Rojewski & Rojewski, 2001, p. 45). Children of these ages have a wider understanding of what it means to be adopted and the implications that come with the adoption. Also, the first exposures to racism and prejudice usually occur during this time. Adolescence can be a very difficult time for intercountry adoptees, because "these young people have to contend with all of the usual challenges of adolescence plus being adopted, and most often being placed in a family that has a different ethnic and racial background than their own" (p. 48). Though all of these stages can be difficult for adoptees, the more open and accepting that they learn to become of their culture and heritage, the easier the time of adjustment will be for them.

The aforementioned issues of adjustment all deal with psychological factors, but there are other developmental adjustments that sometimes need to be addressed. Many intercountry adoptees do suffer from some kind of mental or physical delay when they are adopted. It has been discovered, however, that most "problems, if and when they do arise, are related to preadoptive experiences such as neglect, malnutrition, or separation trauma," not postadoptive factors (Vonk, 2002, p. 4). Even the children who do suffer from these development delays have been found to catch up very quickly once in the United States (p. 5).

22

With all of the steps that have been taken to improve the overall adoption adjustment process, it is no wonder that intercountry adoption from China is generally looked at in such

Comments

22 The last of the objections raised in paragraph six has now been dealt with.

a positive light. Personal experiences of adoptive parents seem to represent these positive findings as well. Christine Bondonese, a **23** physical therapist from Allentown, Pennsylvania, adopted Maia, a baby girl from China, three years ago. Overall, the family's experience has been very positive. They have dealt with many of the adjustment issues mentioned above. Developmental delays were an original concern. Bondonese said, "Maia was 8 months old when we brought her home. However, the doctor told us she was more like 6 months old—she had mild delays—but caught up quickly with no special help." Now 4 years old, Maia has started attending preschool and has adapted very well. Bondonese said that both "socially and academically, she is at the top of her class." To help integrate both cultures, the family belongs to a local chapter of the FCC and keeps many Chinese things in their home, including books and music. Maia has had to adjust to many new things since she was brought to the United States, but Bondonese said that the most important thing they have been able to give her to help in the adjustment process is "lots of love!" (personal communication, November 11, 2002). **24**

Another positive adoption experience can be seen by examining the Lauffer family. John and Johanna Lauffer adopted Janie from China when she was 9 months old. Janie also experienced some developmental delays, but Johanna Lauffer said that "she very quickly caught up, however, and now at the age of 3 is doing great. Her doctor said she is right in line with where she should be." To help integrate the two cultures, the Lauffers brought many things back from China to keep in their home, and they frequently talk about the fact that Janie is adopted and from China. Johanna Lauffer said, "I am not too sure how much she is

Comments

> **23** These transition sentences introduce a short section of original research in the form of interviews with two families who have adopted Chinese children.

> **24** Since conversations and interviews do not contain what APA would consider "recoverable data" such as print or electronic texts, they are cited in the text but are not listed on the reference page.

absorbing now, but we hope it will help" (personal communication, November 15, 2002). It is apparent that most adoptive families face similar issues, but with appropriate parenting and plenty of love, adopted babies from China are able to adapt relatively easily.

While there still are, and probably always will be, opposing views regarding the subject of intercountry adoption from China, the consensus seems to be that the benefits of this type of adoption far outweigh the negatives. With all of the suffering children in the **25** world today, there is no reason why the availability of good homes should be ignored, whether or not they require the children to be adopted into a different country. Many children do suffer some type of developmental delay at their time of arrival, but the vast majority overcome these early delays with few problems. There are also many psychological adjustments that adoptees need to make, but with proper care and attention, these problems can be taken care of just as easily as the developmental delays. Overall, intercountry adoption from China is a positive experience for everyone involved in the process.

Comments

 This return to the basic thesis of the essay (in spite of negatives, intercountry adoption is recommended) signals the beginning of the conclusion. The major points in favor of intercountry adoption are restated.

References   `26`

Bazzoli, F. (2002). International Chinese adoption. *Shared blessings.*   `27`
    Retrieved November 11, 2004, from http://www.night.net/
    rosie/9802-ics-article.html

Dickinson, A. (2002, August 26). Bicultural kids: Parents who adopt
    children of a different ethnicity are enjoying the best of
    both worlds. *Time.* Retrieved November 4, 2004, from Expanded   `28`
    Academic ASAP database.   `29`

Rojewski, J. W., & Rojewski, J. L. (2001). *Intercountry adoption from
    China.* Westport, CT: Bergin & Garvey.

Tessler, R., Gamache, G., & Liu, L. (1999). *West meets East:*   `30`
    Americans adopt Chinese children. Westport, CT: Bergin &
    Garvey.

Transracial and transcultural adoption. (2002, March 3). *National*   `31`
    adoption information clearinghouse. Retrieved November 4,
    2004, from http://www.calib.com/naic/pubs/f_trans.html

Triseliotis, J. (1993). Intercountry adoption: In whose best interest?
    In M. Humphrey & H. Humphrey (Eds.), *Intercountry adoption:*   `32`
    Practical experiences (pp. 119–137). New York: `33`
    Tavistock/Routledge.

Vonk, M. E. (2002, July). Cultural competence for transracial
    adoptive parents. *Social work.* Retrieved November 4, 2004,
    from Expanded Academic ASAP database.

Comments

26 The title of the bibliography page is "References" and is centered.

27 Use the last name but only the initial(s) (not the whole first name) of the author, and follow this with the publication date in parentheses, then a period. An Internet address (URL) is not placed in brackets, but the final period is omitted.

28 In titles (of articles and books, for example), capitalize only the first word, the first word after a colon, and proper nouns. Italicize the titles of books, periodicals, motion pictures, and CDs.

29 This is how to indicate use of a print source that appears in a database.

30 If there is more than one author, all the names and first initials are reversed: last name first, then first name initial or initials.

31 If no author's name appears on the original source, which is often the case with Internet documents, the first item in the entry is the title, followed (like a name) by the date of publication.

32 The article cited here is from an edited volume of essays. Editors' names appear with initial first, then last name.

33 Include all digits in page ranges.